Vikram Seth was born in 1952. He trained as an economist and has lived for several years in the UK, California, China and India. He is the author of the international bestselling novel *A Suitable Boy*, *The Golden Gate: A Novel in Verse*, described by Gore Vidal as 'The Great Californian Novel', *From Heaven Lake: Travels through Sinkiang and Tibet* and four volumes of poetry.

D1077059

Three Chinese Poets

Translations of poems by
Wang Wei, Li Bai and Du Fu

VIKRAM SETH

PHŒNIX

A PHOENIX PAPERBACK

First published in Great Britain
by Faber and Faber Ltd in 1992
This paperback edition published in 1997
by Phoenix,
a division of Orion Books Ltd,
Orion House, 5 Upper St Martin's Lane,
London WC2H 9EA

A CIP catalogue record for this book
is available from the British Library.

ISBN: 1 85799 780 8

Printed and bound in Great Britain by
The Guernsey Press Co. Ltd, Guernsey, C. I.

To Yin Chuang

Professor Chuang, whose stern pen drew
Red rings around my puerile scrawling,
I hope this book appears to you,
If not appealing, not appalling.

Enthusiastic and sardonic,
Exacting, warm, and too soon past,
Your classes, once my daily tonic,
Have borne eccentric fruit at last.

Contents

Acknowledgements

I have consulted a number of books for explanations and original text. I am particularly indebted to *A Little Primer of Du Fu* by David Hawkes (Oxford University Press); *The Poetry of Wang Wei* by Pauline Yu (Indiana University Press); and *Li Tai Bai Quan Ji* (Collected Poems of Li Bai, 2 vols; Xianggang Guangzhi Shuju, i.e. Kwong Chi Book Company, Hong Kong).

I would like to thank my friend Andrew Andreasen, who looked over these translations and made many valuable suggestions; and David Hawkes, who helped me greatly with two of Wang Wei's poems – 'Autumn Nightfall at my Place in the Hills' and 'Ballad of the Peach Tree Spring'.

V.S.

Note on Pronunciation

I have used Pinyin, the standard transliteration of Mandarin Chinese used in mainland China, throughout this book except for well-known names like the Yangtze. In certain older transliterations Li Bai and Du Fu are written as Li Po and Tu Fu.

Most Pinyin consonants sound roughly the same in Chinese as in English. The notable exceptions are: *c* pronounced as 'ts'; *q* as 'chh'; *x* as 'sh'; *z* as 'dz'; *zh* as 'j'.

Most Pinyin vowels sound roughly the same in Chinese as in English, except for *i* in the following syllables: *chi* pronounced as 'chhrr'; *ci* as 'tss'; *ri* as 'rr'; *shi* as 'shrr'; *si* as 'ss'; *zhi* as 'jrr'; *zi* as 'dzz'.

Introduction

Works in translation from languages I do not understand have had as deep an influence on my own writing as works I can read in the original. In some cases the translations have so moved me that I have tried to learn the original language of the work. In others, the form or the spirit of the writing has served as a template for my own inspiration. Life is short, and I doubt I will ever have the delight of reading Pushkin in Russian, Molière in French, or Homer in Greek. But to have at hand Charles Johnston's *Eugene Onegin*, Richard Wilbur's *Tartuffe* or Robert Fitzgerald's *Iliad* has allowed me at least some ingress into worlds that would otherwise be unreachable and most likely unimaginable.

This book is presented as a dual offering – as thanks to those three translators of one generation who have meant so much to me, and as thanks to the three Chinese poets of another generation whose original poems have meant even more. If you, who are reading this, get some pleasure from their poems, it will be in spite of the unremovable barriers of language, which are passable only in part. Much – possibly most – of what they say will be lost, but I hope that even such limited access to the works of Wang Wei, Li Bai and Du Fu as these translations provide will be worthwhile.

The Chinese is one of the richest and certainly the oldest continuous tradition of poetry, stretching back to the *Book of Songs*, which was recorded 2,500 years ago. The three Tang dynasty poets translated in the present volume fall about midway along the line of time stretching from then until now. They lived in the eighth century AD, in an age of great cultural glory interrupted by a disastrous civil war.

The Tang dynasty was founded in 618 by a young man who, after crushing his military rivals and filially installing his father on the throne for eight years, took over as emperor himself under the name of Tai Zong. He recruited talent, honed the administration, expanded China's frontiers and founded an academy at the capital Changan, which became the foremost seat of learning in the world. After his death and that of his somewhat incompetent son and successor, one of Tai Zong's erstwhile concubines installed herself on the throne of China as the Empress Wu. She ruled through intrigue and force for fifteen years until 705, and is one of the most controversial figures in Chinese history. One of her innovations was the inclusion of poetry composition as a compulsory subject in the imperial civil service examinations, which until then had dealt mainly with Confucian texts. This measure was to have a profound influence in contributing to the remarkable reflowering of poetry in the next generation.

Wang Wei, Li Bai and Du Fu grew up under the Emperor Ming Huang, whose long reign began in 713 and lasted for most of their lives. The first decades of his reign were seen both at the time and ever afterwards as a golden age, marked by unprecedented efficiency in government, peace at home and on the borders, economic prosperity and brilliance in the arts. Then, after a long decline, disaster struck.

The emperor, increasingly under the influence of his favourite concubine Yang Guifei, lost all taste for his duties. He became obsessed with extravagant expenditure at court and on military expansion, which he financed by increases in taxation levied on the common people. Honest officials were dismissed, and Yang Guifei's rapacious relatives and favourites were installed in high office. One such favourite was the fat, sinister and capable barbarian general An Lushan, who at first was ingratiatingly jolly and gratefully absorbed the gifts, resources and positions lavished on him. In 755, however, he declared rebellion on the throne, and marched on Changan.

The imperial family and court fled in panic, and An Lushan's forces took control of the capital. It took years to crush the rebellion and the subsidiary rebellions it spawned, and the cost was terrible. Over ten million lives were lost, the economy was devastated, and the country divided into what were virtually military fiefdoms with only nominal imperial sway. The Tang empire staggered on for another century and a half, but its days of grandeur and strength were over.

Tang dynasty China, a huge and diverse country in an age of slow communications, was ruled from the capital by imperial fiat transmitted through and tempered by an élite civil service spread throughout the country. This highly literate élite, recruited largely through rigorous competitive examinations, was both the creator and the major audience for poetry. The ability to compose poetry was considered to be one of the accomplishments of a scholar-gentleman even before it was made a compulsory subject in the examinations; afterwards it became a necessity. It was moreover accepted as a profound medium not only of self-expression but of the indirect expression of moral or political philosophy.

The world into which the three almost exactly contemporary poets – Wang Wei, Li Bai and Du Fu – were born can be sensed in many specific aspects of their poetry; for example, their stance with respect to the court and affairs of state, and the value they placed on friendship in a world of slow transport and great distances, where parting from a friend held the real possibility of never seeing him again. There is a large common zone of sentiment among the three – their appreciation of music, their acute perception of nature, their bent towards nostalgia.

But despite this and despite the fact that many of the poems of these three poets are in identical forms, their personalities and the spirit of their writing could not have been more different. The standard trichotomy of Wang Wei as Buddhist recluse, Li Bai as Taoist immortal and Du Fu as Confucian sage has been rejected by some critics as unsubtle and artificial, but it can act as a clarifying approximation for those approaching Chinese poetry of this period for the first time. The centre of gravity of their work, the characteristic emphasis of their most characteristic poems, is distinct and individual.

Wang Wei's typical mood is that of aloneness, quiet, a retreat into nature and Buddhism. What one associates with him are running water, evening and dawn, bamboo, the absence of men's voices. The word 'empty' is almost his signature. Li Bai's poetry sparkles with zest, impulsiveness, exuberance, even at the risk of bombast and imbalance. Sword, horse, wine, gold, the moon, the Milky Way and impossibly large numbers are recurring features of his work. He attempts alchemically to transmute life through the intoxication of poetry or music or wine into delight and forgetfulness. Du Fu's poetry is informed by deeply suggestive and often sad reflections on society, history, the state and his own disturbed times, all central concerns of Confucianism. But what especially endears him to the Chinese is his wry self-deprecation combined with an intense compassion for oppressed or dispossessed people of every kind in a time of poverty, famine and war.

Wang Wei, the first of the three poets translated here, was born into a distinguished literary family on his mother's side; his father was a local official. He was a prodigy – an accomplished musician, artist, calligrapher and poet who wrote the classic 'Ballad of the Peach Tree Spring' at seventeen. When he and his younger brother Wang Jin went up to the capital they were readily absorbed into aristocratic society. Wang Wei passed the imperial examinations at twenty-three. He was appointed to the post of Assistant Secretary for Music, but soon afterwards, probably for some small dereliction of duty, was transferred to a minor provincial post, where he served for several years before resigning and returning to the capital. He bought an estate in the hills on the Wang River about thirty miles away from Changan. Here he lived whenever he was on holiday or out of office, and its landscape was the source of much of his painting and poetry. Not long afterwards, Wang Wei's wife died. He was under thirty, and childless, but he never married again.

He filled a series of posts, none of which seem to have involved him as much as the calm pleasures of his country estate: nature, friends and Buddhist philosophy were his preoccupations. He survived the recurrent court intrigues unscathed; this was probably because he was not much interested in what went on at court even though he wrote the occasional court poem upon request.

When rebellion struck and An Lushan established his bloody rule in Changan, Wang Wei, after some resistance, accepted office under him. His dear friend and fellow poet Pei Di, fifteen years his junior, managed to visit him during the occupation, and Wang Wei recited to him a poem touching upon his sorrow and dismay at the recent events. When the rebellion was crushed and imperial control re-established in Changan, it was very likely this poem together with the intercession of his brother Wang Jin – who had followed the emperor into exile and established impeccable loyalist credentials – that saved him from execution.

Wang Wei died four years later at the age of sixty-one. After his death Wang Jin, then prime minister, ordered that his scattered poems be collected, but many – possibly most – of his poems (like those of Li Bai and Du Fu) have been lost. As for his paintings – and Wang Wei was at least as famous in his lifetime for his painting as for his poetry – nothing remains except much later copies (several times removed) of his work. It was said of him by a later poet, Su Dongpo, that 'there was poetry in his painting and painting in his poetry'. His landscapes, like his poetry, are said to have embodied a sense of distance, space and the pervading presence of 'emptiness'.

Li Bai was born in Chinese Turkestan in 701 and moved to Sichuan around the age of five. He travelled a great deal throughout China, never sat the imperial examinations or held a post for long, and rarely mentioned specific contemporary events in his poetry. As a result not a great deal is known about his life or his exact movements.

He is known to have been married several times, to have had children, and to have made a great impression on his contemporaries as a paradigm of the intoxicated and impulsive poet with his flashing eyes and great iconoclastic energy. He was interested in alchemy and in Taoism.

In his early forties he was presented to the emperor in Changan and given a position in the Imperial Academy, but this did not last long; he was unseated in a court intrigue. When the An Lushan rebellion broke out he was in his mid-fifties. He left for the south and entered the service of Prince Yong, but the prince was himself later killed by the emperor who feared that he might usurp his throne. Li Bai too was implicated in the plot and exiled to the south-west. Before he got there, however, he was pardoned, and so continued his wanderings. He died in 762 while visiting a relative, a famous calligrapher.

The vigour and flamboyance of much of Li Bai's poetry hides a deep core of loneliness. He achieved great fame in his lifetime, and seems only on occasion to have known want; for the most part those who met him felt honoured to provide him with generous hospitality. But he saw himself as a man in heroic and romantic opposition to the universe and was torn by nostalgia. He never settled down, and the restless energy of his life found its counterpart both in the speed with which he set down his compositions and in their propulsive sweep. His longer poems in irregular metres are particularly heady and daring, and provide a sense of escape into a height beyond the dross and boredom of daily life. Some of his nature poetry – for example, 'The Road to Shu' – is tumultuous, almost at times bizarre, in its dramatic detail.

Though Li Bai was born in the same year as Wang Wei and died just a year before him, it is not clear whether they ever met. They did however have a common friend in the poet Meng Haoran, twelve years their senior, and each wrote poems addressed to him or to his memory. Meng Haoran could be said to have combined in his work two threads of Chinese nature poetry – the quietistic stream which was to find its most intense expression in the poetry of Wang Wei, and the sense of natural grandeur that found expression in some of the poetry of Li Bai.

Du Fu's attitude to nature is somewhat different from that of either Wang Wei or Li Bai. He sees nature not as retreat or drama but as an emotional or moral entity set in juxtaposition to human life and human events, whether in sympathy or antipathy. The noble cypress that is not uprooted by violent storms, the flowers that insist on returning in spring to a devastated war-stricken country – these appear to him to be intimately tied through either consciousness or heedlessness to human vicissitudes and griefs.

Du Fu experienced a great deal of both during his life. He was born in 712 into a distinguished but not wealthy family; his grandfather was a famous poet. Although – like both Wang Wei and Li Bai, his seniors by a decade – he displayed great literary promise in his teens, he failed the imperial examinations in his early twenties, and was to fail them again in his mid-thirties. In the meantime he travelled widely in south-central China, visiting historical sites and meeting (among other poets) Li Bai, one of his great heroes, who was to become a lifelong friend. In 752 Du Fu took a special examination in the capital, and failed yet again.

For Du Fu, repeated lack of success in the examinations was a triple failure. He needed the salary of an official: unlike some other poets he had not been able to obtain economic support through a personal patron, and had to live apart from his wife and children, whom he could not afford to keep in the capital. Secondly, his natural ambition for office was continually thwarted. Thirdly, his wish to be of use to his country was frustrated. For a man bred in Confucian traditions, unselfish service to the emperor, to the state and to the people was what gave life meaning. Li Bai and Wang Wei, each in his own way, felt that the essential purposes of life lay elsewhere; this was not possible for Du Fu.

In 755, Du Fu was awarded a minor office low in the official hierarchy. But soon thereafter the An Lushan rebellion broke out, and in 756 the capital fell to the rebels. Du Fu was not in Changan at the time but arrived there later; it is said that he was captured by the rebels and brought to Changan, but the facts are unclear. Many of his greatest poems date from this period; these include 'Grieving for the Young Prince' and 'Spring Scene in Time of War'. He was again separated from his family. One of his children had already died of starvation, and once more his family was faced with penury.

Du Fu managed to leave Changan and join the court in exile. In 757 he was appointed to a higher rank as a reward for his loyalty. This he lost shortly afterwards; his defence of a general who had lost a battle caused him to fall out of imperial favour, and he was exiled to Shaanxi. A couple of years later he left for Sichuan, where in semi-retirement, in the last decade of his life, he wrote over half of the 1,450 poems of his that survive. In 765 he undertook a journey down the Yangtze. He fell ill on the way and was forced to remain at Kuizhou for two years. In 768 he continued towards Henan, where he had been born; but in 770, while still travelling, he died.

Neither Du Fu's personality nor his poetry made a great impression on most of his contemporaries. Unlike Li Bai and Wang Wei, he was not included in major poetry anthologies for several generations after his death. But from before the turn of the millennium and continuously since then he has been considered to be one of China's greatest poets. His feeling for the things of consequence of his times, his realism and honesty, the richness of his technique and language, the moral force of his writing, his affection and concern for those around him and his sense of fun have ensured immortality for the poet who received meagre literary acclaim in his lifetime. Even his unsuccess in office, his long periods of unemployment, can with time be seen in a different light. As with that other diligent bureaucrat Chaucer, we would not have as much of his work as we do if he had escaped what must have seemed to him fallow and frustrating times.

Partly as a matter of interest, and partly in order to illustrate those effects attained by Chinese poetry that are lost in these translations, it may be worthwhile briefly to analyse one of the original poems included in this book. A quick look at the longer poems of Du Fu or Li Bai shows that several forms using irregular line-lengths were popular during this period. However, the most commonly used of all forms for several centuries – more standard even than the sonnet in Europe – was an eight-line regular form with the same number of syllables in each line throughout the poem, either five or seven. The second, fourth, sixth and eighth lines of the octet rhymed with one another, thus reinforcing the basic division of four couplets within the octet. (Sometimes the first line rhymed with them as well.)

In the strict or 'regulated' form of the octet that increased in popularity during the Tang there were two additional features. One was a prescribed sequence of so-called 'tones' for successive syllables of the poem once a certain pattern had been chosen. In classical Chinese, syllables – each exactly one written character long – were classified into tones depending on the direction of pitch of the sound. (The meaning of the syllable depended then, as now, upon this pitch-direction.) The pattern of tones in the regulated octet set up expectations and provided musical satisfactions that are impossible to provide in a non-tonal language like English. This is part of what is necessarily lost in translation.

The other feature was exact grammatical parallelism and contrast of meaning between lines three and four, and again between lines five and six. This parallelism within each of the second and third couplets is a particular pleasure of the Chinese regulated octet, but in my translations I have often let natural English syntax override strict parallelism in order to avoid what might otherwise emerge as a choppy or a rigid rendering. In the example of the poem by Wang Wei given below it should be borne in mind that Chinese parts of speech are not the same as English ones, and that the requirement of grammatical parallelism has in fact been strictly adhered to in the middle couplets. (As it happens, in this particular poem parallelism holds within each of the four couplets, but that is not a requirement of the form.)

Much of the pleasure of rhymed and metred poetry depends, obviously enough, on rhyme and metre; and these are intrinsic to the enjoyment of classical Chinese verse. This is true even though over the centuries most characters have changed in pronunciation, not always consistently with each other, and as a result what were once exact rhymes are now sometimes half-rhymes or less. I felt in my translations that wherever I could I should maintain rhyme, and also wherever possible retain a sense of the regularity or irregularity of the metrical movement. The joy of poetry for me lies not so much in transcending or escaping from the so-called bonds of artifice or constraint as in using them to enhance the power of what is being said.

With so much by way of general explication, I would invite the reader to look at 'Living in the Hills: Impromptu Verses' by Wang Wei – reproduced on the following page with its eight-by-five grid of characters, their pronunciation in modern Mandarin Chinese, their meaning, and a line-by-line prose translation.

This is an immensely simple poem, yet one which, once read, I have never been able to forget. To compare the incomparable, if the difficulty of translating Wang Wei is akin to the difficulty of playing Mozart, the difficulty of translating Du Fu with his rich counterpoint of historical allusion can be compared to that of playing Bach. As for translating the wild and romantic Li Bai – it is rather like playing Beethoven, often full of sound and fury, signifying (usually) a great deal. But in each poem, as important as the texture or tone of the work is the exact content of what is being said – and the translator's task is not to improvise cadenzas in the spirit of the piece but to stick, as tellingly as he can, to the score.

There is a school of translation that believes that one can safely ignore many of the actual words of a poem once one has drunk deeply of its spirit. An approximate rendering invigorated by a sense of poetic inspiration becomes the aim. The idea is that if the final product reads well as a poem, all is well: a good poem exists where none existed before. I should mention that the poems in this book are not intended as transcreations

1. 寂　寞　掩　柴　扉
JÍ　MÒ　YǍN　CHÁI　FĒI　[Rhyme]
lonely　　close　brushwood　door
Lonely, I close my brushwood door.

2. 蒼　茫　對　落　暉
CĀNG　MÁNG　DÙI　LÙO　HŪI　[Rhyme]
vast/misty　　face　falling　light/brilliance
I face the vast expanse as the sunset falls.

3. 鶴　巢　松　樹　徧
HÉ　CHÁO　SŌNG　SHÙ　BIÀN
cranes　nest　pine　tree　everywhere
Cranes nest everywhere in the pine trees.

4. 人　訪　蓽　門　稀
RÉN　FĂNG　BÌ　MÉN　XĪ　[Rhyme]
men　visit　wicker　gate　few
I have few visitors at my wicker gate.

5. 嫩　竹　含　新　粉
NÈN　ZHÚ　HÁN　XĪN　FĚN
tender　bamboo　holds　new　powder
The tender bamboo holds new powder.

6. 紅　蓮　落　故　衣
HÓNG　LIÁN　LÙO　GǓ　YĪ　[Rhyme]
red　lotus　sheds　old　clothes
Red lotuses shed their old clothes.

7. 渡　頭　燈　火　起
DÙ　TÓU　DĒNG　HǓO　QĬ
at the ford　　lantern fires　rise
Lantern fires are lit at the ford.

8. 處　處　採　菱　歸
CHÙ　CHÙ　CǍI　LÍNG　GŪI　[Rhyme]
everywhere　water-chestnut pickers　return home
Everywhere water-chestnut pickers go home.

Grammatically parallel pair of lines

Grammatically parallel pair of lines

or free translations in this sense, attempts to use the originals as trampolines from which to bounce off on to poems of my own. The famous translations of Ezra Pound, compounded as they are of ignorance of Chinese and valiant self-indulgence, have remained before me as a warning of what to shun. I have preferred mentors who, like the three translators I mentioned before, admit the primacy of the original and attempt fidelity to it. Like them, I have tried not to compromise the meaning of the actual words of the poems, though I have often failed. Even in prose the associations of a word or an image in one language do not slip readily into another. The loss is still greater in poetry, where each word or image carries a heavier charge of association, and where the exigencies of form leave less scope for choice and manoeuvre. But if it is felt that the limited access to the worlds of these poems that translation can reasonably hope to provide has been given, I will be more than happy.

王 維　　　　　　　Wang Wei

Deer Park

Empty hills, no man in sight –
Just echoes of the voice of men.
In the deep wood reflected light
Shines on the blue-green moss again.

Birdsong Brook

Idly I watch cassia flowers fall.
Still is the night, empty the hill in Spring.
Up comes the moon, startling the mountain birds.
Once in a while in the Spring brook they sing.

Lady Xi

No present royal favour could efface
The memory of the love that once she knew.
Seeing a flower filled her eyes with tears.
She did not speak a word to the King of Chu.

Grieving for Meng Haoran

I will not ever see my friend again.
Day after day Han waters eastward flow.
Even if I asked of the old man, the hills
And rivers would seem empty in Caizhou.

Remembering My Brothers in Shandong on the
Double-Ninth Festival

Alone, a stranger in a distant province –
At festivals I'm homesick through and through.
In my mind's eye, my brothers climb the mountain,
Each carrying dogwood – but there's one too few.

The Pleasures of the Country

Peach blossom's red; again it holds night rain.
Willows are green, clad once more in spring mist.
The houseboy's not yet swept the fallen flowers.
The orioles chirp, but don't wake my hill guest.

Autumn Nightfall at my Place in the Hills

In the empty mountains, after recent rain,
A sense of Fall comes with the evening air.
The moon is bright and shines between the pines.
Over the stones the spring-fed stream runs clear.
Bamboos rustle: washerwomen go home.
Lotuses stir: fishing boats make their way.
At its own will, the scent of Spring has gone.
But you, 'O prince of friends', of course may stay.

Zhongnan Retreat

In middle age I'm quite drawn to the Way.
Here by the hills I've built a home. I go
– Whenever the spirit seizes me – alone
To see the spots that other folk don't know.
I walk to the head of the stream, sit down, and watch
For when the clouds rise. On the forest track
By chance I meet an old man, and we talk
And laugh, and I don't think of going back.

In Answer to Vice-Magistrate Zhang

Late in my life I only care for quiet.
A million pressing tasks, I let them go.
I look at myself; I have no long range plans.
To go back to the forest is all I know.
Pine breeze: I ease my belt. Hill moon: I strum
My lute. You ask – but I can say no more
About success or failure than the song
The fisherman sings, which comes to the deep shore.

Living in the Hills: Impromptu Verses

I close my brushwood door in solitude
And face the vast sky as late sunlight falls.
The pine trees: cranes are nesting all around.
My wicker gate: a visitor seldom calls.
The tender bamboo's dusted with fresh powder.
Red lotuses strip off their former bloom.
Lamps shine out at the ford, and everywhere
The water-chestnut pickers wander home.

Lament for Yin Yao

How long can one man's lifetime last?
In the end we return to formlessness.
I think of you, waiting to die.
A thousand things cause me distress —

Your kind old mother's still alive.
Your only daughter's only ten.
In the vast chilly wilderness
I hear the sounds of weeping men.

Clouds float into a great expanse.
Birds fly but do not sing in flight.
How lonely are the travellers.
Even the sun shines cold and white.

Alas, when you still lived, and asked
To study non-rebirth with me,
My exhortations were delayed —
And so the end came, fruitlessly.

All your old friends have brought you gifts
But for your life these too are late.
I've failed you in more ways than one.
Weeping, I walk back to my gate.

Ballad of the Peach Tree Spring

A fisherman sailed up-river; he loved the hills in Spring.
On either bank of the old ford stood peach trees blossoming.
He stared at the red trees. The miles passed; unaware,
He reached the green creek's end but saw no human anywhere.
A gap – a hidden path twisted and turned about –
Then suddenly among the hills a vast plain opened out.
From far, a host of clouds and trees – but as he neared
Among bamboos and scattered flowers a thousand homes
            appeared.
Woodcutters with Han names and surnames passed them on.
The villagers still wore the clothes of Qin times, long since
            gone.
Together all of them now lived at Wuling Spring,
Tilling their gardens and their fields away from everything.
Moon bright below the pines – their houses all lay quiet.
When the sun rose among the clouds, roosters and dogs ran
            riot.
A visitor from the world! They gathered round and vied
To ask him home and question him on how things were
            outside.
From village lanes at dawn they swept the flowers away.
Woodsmen and fishermen rowed home towards the close of
            day.
At first they'd come to flee the world and, some maintain,
Had then become immortals and decided to remain.
From these ravines who'd guess human affairs exist? –
And from the world you'd only see blank mountains cloaked
            in mist.
He did not think such realms were hard to hear or see;
His heart, still dusty with the world, longed for his own
            country.

He went out through the cave, not heeding stream or hill,
To take his leave from home and then return here at his will.
Certain he could not lose what he had just passed through,
How could he know when he returned the landscape would
                                                    look new?
He'd gone into deep hills – but nothing else was clear.
How often into cloudy woods do green creeks disappear?
All over every stream in Spring peach blossom lies.
Who can discern where he should seek the spring of paradise?

李　白　　　　　　　　　Li Bai

In the Quiet Night

The floor before my bed is bright:
Moonlight – like hoarfrost – in my room.
I lift my head and watch the moon.
I drop my head and think of home.

A Song of Qiu-pu

The Qiu-pu shore teems with white gibbons.
They leap and bounce like flying snow.
They tug their young down from the branches
To drink and play with the moonglow.

The Waterfall at Lu Shan

In sunshine, Censer Peak breathes purple mist.
A jutting stream, the cataract hangs in spray
Far off, then plunges down three thousand feet –
As if the sky had dropped the Milky Way.

Question and Answer in the Mountains

They ask me why I live in the green mountains.
I smile and don't reply; my heart's at ease.
Peach blossoms flow downstream, leaving no trace –
And there are other earths and skies than these.

Seeing Meng Haoran off to Yangzhou

Yellow Crane Terrace: my old friend bids me goodbye.
To Yangzhou in the mists and flowers of Spring he goes.
His single sail's far shadow melts in the blue void.
All I see is the sky to which the Yangtze flows.

Parting at a Wineshop in Nanjing

Breeze bearing willow-cotton fills the shop with scent.
A Wu girl, pouring wine, exhorts us to drink up.
We Nanjing friends are here to see each other off.
Those who must go, and those who don't, each drains his
cup.
Go ask the Yangtze, which of these two sooner ends:
Its waters flowing east – the love of parting friends.

Listening to a Monk from Shu Playing the Lute

The monk from Shu with his green lute-case walked
Westward down Emei Shan, and at the sound
Of the first notes he strummed for me I heard
A thousand valleys' rustling pines resound.
My heart was cleansed, as if in flowing water.
In bells of frost I heard the resonance die.
Dusk came unnoticed over the emerald hills
And autumn clouds layered the darkening sky.

The Mighty Eunuchs' Carriages

The mighty eunuchs' carriages
Raise a great swirl of dust that shrouds
The fields in darkness though it's noon.
What wealth! Their mansions touch the clouds.

They bump into a cockfight now.
Bright canopies! Superb headgear!
A double rainbow tints their breath.
Folk by the roadside quake with fear.

Since Xu You washed his ears in shame
When offered a place at court, who can
Distinguish between Yao and Zhi –
The brigand and the virtuous man?

Drinking Alone with the Moon

A pot of wine among the flowers.
I drink alone, no friend with me.
I raise my cup to invite the moon.
He and my shadow and I make three.

The moon does not know how to drink;
My shadow mimes my capering;
But I'll make merry with them both –
And soon enough it will be Spring.

I sing – the moon moves to and fro.
I dance – my shadow leaps and sways.
Still sober, we exchange our joys.
Drunk – and we'll go our separate ways.

Let's pledge – beyond human ties – to be friends,
And meet where the Silver River ends.

Bring in the Wine

The waters of the Yellow River come down from the sky,
Never once returning as towards the sea they flow.
The mirrors of high palaces are sad with once-bright hair:
Though silken-black at morning it has changed by night to
                                                    snow.
Fulfil your wishes in this life, exhaust your every whim
And never raise an empty golden goblet to the moon.
Fate's loaded me with talent and it must be put to use!
Scatter a thousand coins – they'll all come winging
                                        homeward soon.
Cook a sheep, slaughter an ox – and for our further pleasure
Let's drink three hundred cups of wine down in a single
                                                measure.
        So here's to you, Dan Qiu –
        And Master Cen, drink up.
        Bring in, bring in the wine –
        Pour on, cup after cup.
        I'll sing a song for you –
        So lend your ears and hear me through.
Bells and drums and feasts and jade are all esteemed in vain:
Just let me be forever drunk and never be sober again.
The sages and the virtuous men are all forgotten now.
It is the drinkers of the world whose names alone remain.
Chen Wang, the prince and poet, once at a great banquet
                                                    paid
Ten thousand for a cask of wine with laughter wild and free.
How can you say, my host, that you have fallen short of
                                                    cash?

You've got to buy more wine and drink it face to face with me.
      My furs so rare –
      My dappled mare –
Summon the boy to go and get the choicest wine for these
And we'll dissolve the sorrows of a hundred centuries.

The Road to Shu is Hard

Ah! it's fearsome – oh! it's high!
The road to Shu is hard, harder than climbing to the sky.
      The kings Can Cong and Yu Fu
      Founded long ago the land of Shu.
      Then for forty-eight thousand years
      Nothing linked it to the Qin frontiers.
      White Star Peak blocked the western way.
A bird-track tried to cut across to Mount Emei –
And only when the earth shook, hills collapsed, and brave
                           men died
Did cliff-roads and sky-ladders join it to the world outside.
Above – high peaks turn back the dragon-chariot of the sun.
Below – great whirlpools turn around the waves that rush
                           and stun.
      Not even yellow cranes can fly across –
      Even the clambering apes are at a loss.
      At Green Mud Ridge the path coils to and fro:
Nine twists for every hundred steps – up a sheer cliff we go.
The traveller, touching the stars, looks upwards, scared out
                           of his wits.
He clutches his heart with a deep sigh – down on the ground
                           he sits!

Sir, from this journey to the West, will you return some day?
How can you hope to climb the crags along this fearful way?
Mournful birds in ancient trees – you'll hear no other sound
Of life: the male bird follows his mate as they fly round and
                           round.
      You'll hear the cuckoo call in the moonlight,
        Sad that the mountain's bare at night.

The road to Shu is hard, harder than climbing to the sky.
Just speak these words to someone's face – you'll see its
                                        colour fly.
A hand's breadth from the sky peaks join to crown a
                                        precipice
Where withered pines, bent upside down, lean over the
                                        abyss.
Swift rapids, wrestling cataracts descend in roaring spasms,
Pound cliffs, boil over rocks, and thunder through ten
                                thousand chasms.
        To face such danger and such fear,
Alas, from such a distance, Sir, what could have brought
                                you here?
        Dagger Peak is high and steep –
        Even a single man can keep
        The pass from thousands – though he may
Become a wolf or jackal – and betray.
By day we dread the savage tiger's claws,
        By night the serpent's jaws,
    Its sharp, blood-sucking fangs bared when
It mows down like hemp stalks the lives of men.
    Though Chengdu is a pleasure dome,
    Better to quickly turn back home.
The road to Shu is hard, harder than climbing to the sky.
Leaning, I stare into the west and utter a long sigh.

杜 甫   Du Fu

Thoughts while Travelling at Night

Light breeze on the fine grass.
I stand alone at the mast.

Stars lean on the vast wild plain.
Moon bobs in the Great River's spate.

Letters have brought no fame.
Office? Too old to obtain.

Drifting, what am I like?
A gull between earth and sky.

Spring Scene in Time of War

The state lies ruined; hills and streams survive.
Spring in the city; grass and leaves now thrive.
Moved by the times the flowers shed their dew.
The birds seem startled; they hate parting too.
The steady beacon fires are three months old.
A word from home is worth a ton of gold.
I scratch my white hair, which has grown so thin
It soon won't let me stick my hatpin in.

Moonlit Night

In Fuzhou, far away, my wife is watching
The moon alone tonight, and my thoughts fill
With sadness for my children, who can't think
Of me here in Changan; they're too young still.
Her cloud-soft hair is moist with fragrant mist.
In the clear light her white arms sense the chill.
When will we feel the moonlight dry our tears,
Leaning together on our window-sill?

The Visitor

South and north of my house lies springtime water,
And only flocks of gulls come every day.
The flower path's unswept: no guests. The gate
Is open: you're the first to come this way.
The market's far: my food is nothing special.
The wine, because we're poor, is an old brew –
But if you wish I'll call my ancient neighbour
Across the fence to drink it with us two.

Thoughts on an Ancient Site: The Temple of Zhu-ge Liang

The name of Zhu-ge Liang resounds through time.
The statesman's likeness awes: revered, sublime.
The empire, split in three, curbed his great aim
But not the soaring feather of his fame.
He equalled Yi and Lü; if he'd gained power
Great names like Cao and Xiao would have ranked lower –
But time would not restore the Han again.
He died, devoid of hope, his plans all vain.

The Chancellor of Shu

The Chancellor of Shu, where may his shrine be seen?
Among dense cypress trees beyond the city walls.
Unviewed against the steps the grass greets spring in green.
Sweet-voiced, leaf-screened, unheard, a yellow oriole calls.
Begged thrice to plan the world, he finally complied.
He founded or maintained two reigns with faithfulness.
Before his armies proved victorious he died.
Heroic men shed tears to think of his distress.

An Autumn Meditation

I've heard it said Changan is like a chessboard, where
Failure and grief is all these hundred years have brought.
Mansions of princes and high nobles have new lords.
New officers are capped and robed for camp and court.

North on the passes gold drums thunder. To the west
Horses and chariots rush dispatches and reports.
Dragon and fish are still, the autumn river's cold.
My ancient land and times of peace come to my thoughts.

Dreaming of Li Bai

The pain of death's farewells grows dim.
The pain of life's farewells stays new.
Since you were exiled to Jiangnan
— Plague land — I've had no news of you.

Proving how much you're in my thoughts,
Old friend, you've come into my dreams.
I thought you still were in the law's
Tight net — but you've grown wings, it seems.

I fear yours is no living soul.
How could it make this distant flight?
You came: the maple woods were green.
You left: the pass was black with night.

The sinking moonlight floods my room.
Still hoping for your face, I stare.
The water's deep, the waves are wide.
Watch out for water-dragons there.

To Wei Ba, who has Lived Away from the Court

Like stars that rise when the other has set,
For years we two friends have not met.
How rare it is then that tonight
We once more share the same lamplight.
Our youth has quickly slipped away
And both of us are turning grey.
Old friends have died, and with a start
We hear the sad news, sick at heart.
How could I, twenty years before,
Know that I'd be here at your door?
When last I left, so long ago,
You were unmarried. In a row
Suddenly now your children stand,
Welcome their father's friend, demand
To know his home, his town, his kin –
Till they're chased out to fetch wine in.
Spring chives are cut in the night rain
And steamed rice mixed with yellow grain.
To mark the occasion, we should drink
Ten cups of wine straight off, you think –
But even ten can't make me high,
So moved by your old love am I.
The mountains will divide our lives,
Each to his world, when day arrives.

The Old Cypress Tree at the Temple of Zhu-ge Liang

Before the temple stands an ancient cypress tree.
Its boughs are bronze, its roots like heavy boulders lie.
Its massive frosty girth of bark is washed by rain.
Its jet-black head rears up a mile to greet the sky.

Princes and ministers have paid their debt to time.
The people love the tree as they did long ago.
The clouds' breath joins it to the long mists of Wu Gorge.
It shares the moon's chill with the high white peaks of snow.

Last year the road wound east, past my old home, near where
Both Zhu-ge Liang and his First Ruler shared one shrine.
There too great cypresses stretched over the ancient plain,
And through wrecked doors I glimpsed dim paintwork and
design.

But this lone tree, spread wide, root-coiled to earth, has held
Its sky-high place round which fierce blasts of wind are hurled.
Nothing but Providence could keep it here so long.
Its straightness marks the work of what once made the world.

If a great hall collapsed, the oxen sent to drag
Rafters from this vast tree would turn round in dismay.
It needs no craftsman's skills, this wonder of the world.
Even if felled, who could haul such a load away?

Although its bitter heart is marred by swarms of ants,
Among its scented leaves bright phoenixes collect.
Men of high aims, who live obscure, do not despair.
The great are always paid in disuse and neglect.

A Fine Lady

There is a lady, matchless in her beauty.
An empty valley's where she dwells, obscure.
Her family, she says, was once a good one.
She lives with grass and trees now, spent and poor.

When lately there was chaos in the heartlands
And at the rebels' hands her brothers died,
Their high rank failed them, as did her entreaties:
Their flesh and bones remained unsanctified.

The busy world, as fickle as a lamp-flame,
Hates what has had its day or is decayed.
The faithless man to whom she once was married
Keeps a new woman, beautiful as jade.

Those trees whose leaves curl up at night sense evening.
Without its mate a mandarin duck can't sleep.
He only sees the smile of his new woman.
How can he then hear his old woman weep?

Among the mountains, spring-fed streams run clearly.
Leaving the mountains, they are soiled with dross.
Her maid has sold her pearls and is returning.
To mend the thatch they drag the vines across.

Her hands are often full of bitter cypress.
The flowers she picks don't go to grace her hair.
She rests against tall bamboo trees at nightfall.
The weather's cold and her blue sleeves threadbare.

Grieving for the Young Prince

From Changan walls white-headed crows took flight
And cawed upon the Western Gate at night –
Then on officials' roofs they pecked and cawed
To warn them to escape the barbarian horde.
The gold whips broke, so hard were they applied.
The exhausted horses galloped till they died.
The court fled, panicked – those they could not find
Of the imperial line were left behind.

Below his waist, blue coral, glints of jade –
I see a young prince, weeping and afraid
By the cross-roads. Although he won't confess
His name to me he begs in his distress
To be my slave. Thorn scrub he's hidden in
For months has left no untorn shred of skin –
But the imperial nose betrays his birth:
The Dragon's seed is not the seed of earth.

Wolves, jackals roam the city. In the wild
The Dragon and his court remain exiled.
Take care, dear Prince. I daren't speak long with you,
But for your sake will pause a breath or two.

Last night the east wind's blood-stench stained the air
And camels filled the former capital's square.
The Shuofang veterans, bright in their array,
How bold they seemed once, how inane today.
I hear the Son of Heaven has abdicated,
And in the North the Khan, it is related,
And each of his brave warriors slashed his face
– So moved were they by the imperial grace –

And swore to wipe this great dishonour out.
But we must mind our words, with spies about.
Alas, poor Prince, be careful. May the power
Of the Five Tombs protect you hour by hour.

Ballad of the Army Carts

Carts rattle and squeak,
Horses snort and neigh –
Bows and arrows at their waists, the conscripts march away.
Fathers, mothers, children, wives run to say goodbye.
The Xianyang Bridge in clouds of dust is hidden from the eye.
They tug at them and stamp their feet, weep, and obstruct
their way.

The weeping rises to the sky.
Along the road a passer-by
Questions the conscripts. They reply:

They mobilize us constantly. Sent northwards at fifteen
To guard the River, we were forced once more to volunteer,
Though we are forty now, to man the western front this year.
The headman tied our headcloths for us when we first left
here.
We came back white-haired – to be sent again to the frontier.
Those frontier posts could fill the sea with the blood of
those who've died,
But still the Martial Emperor's aims remain unsatisfied.
In county after county to the east, Sir, don't you know,
In village after village only thorns and brambles grow.
Even if there's a sturdy wife to wield the plough and hoe,
The borders of the fields have merged, you can't tell east
from west.
It's worse still for the men from Qin, as fighters they're the
best –
And so, like chickens or like dogs, they're driven to and fro.

Though you are kind enough to ask,
Dare we complain about our task?
Take, Sir, this winter. In Guanxi

The troops have not yet been set free.
The district officers come to press
The land tax from us nonetheless.
But, Sir, how can we possibly pay?
Having a son's a curse today.
Far better to have daughters, get them married –
A son will lie lost in the grass, unburied.
Why, Sir, on distant Qinghai shore
The bleached ungathered bones lie year on year.
New ghosts complain, and those who died before
Weep in the wet grey sky and haunt the ear.

Notes to Poems

1 Lady Xi
The King of Chu in the seventh century BC defeated the ruler of Xi and took his wife. She had children by him but never spoke to him.

Fourteen centuries later Wang Wei, then twenty years old, wrote this poem in the following circumstances. One of his patrons, a prince, had acquired the wife of a cake-seller. A year later he asked her if she still loved her husband, and she gave no answer. The man was sent for, and when she saw him her eyes filled with tears.

This took place before a small but distinguished literary gathering, and the prince, moved, asked for poems on the subject. Wang Wei's poem was finished first, and when it was read out, everyone else agreed it was pointless to try to write something better.

The prince reportedly returned the cake-seller's wife to her husband.

2 Autumn Nightfall at my Place in the Hills
The reason for Wang Wei's unseasonable merging of the disappearance of spring with the onset of autumn is that he is referring to and contrasting his lines with an ancient poem that was well-known to Tang dynasty readers. In that poem, while attempting to draw a reclusive gentleman (the so-called 'prince') back to civilization, the anonymous poet mentions the dense spring grass as one of the features of the mountain wilderness that the recluse has retreated to, and where he 'should not stay long'.

3 Lament for Yin Yao
In Buddhism, 'non-rebirth' (*wu-sheng*: literally, non-birth) denotes nirvana or liberation from the cycle of eternal rebirth.

4 Ballad of the Peach Tree Spring
If the character for 'woodcutter' in line 9 is a miscopying of the original character for 'fisherman' – which is possible since the two written characters are quite similar – a reading would result which accords far better with Wang Wei's original prose source for the legend. Lines 9 and 10 could then read:
'The fisherman was the first to bring news of the Han.
The folk here still wore clothes in vogue before that age began.'

5 In the Quiet Night
This is the well-known, well-loved and much-quoted version of the quatrain. In the version of the poem found in most anthologies of Li Bai, the moon in line 3 is specified as a hill moon or mountain moon.

6 Listening to a Monk from Shu Playing the Lute
See note 10.

7 *Drinking Alone with the Moon*
The Silver River is the Chinese name for the Milky Way.

8 *The Road to Shu is Hard*
See note 10.

9 *Thoughts while Travelling at Night*
The Great River is the Yangtze.

10 *Thoughts on an Ancient Site: The Temple of Zhu-ge Liang*
Shu is the name for the ancient kingdom approximating modern-day
Sichuan, and is a term still used to refer to that province. It consists mainly
of a vast, fertile, densely populated, mountain-ringed basin in the upper
reaches of the Yangtze. In Tang times it was connected to the outside world
either by precipitous mountain paths or via the three gorges (including the
long Wu Gorge) that led to the middle and lower reaches of the Yangtze.

The legend, ancient even in Tang times, goes that a king of Qin promised
his five daughters to a king of Shu, and five brave men of Shu were sent to
fetch them. On the way back they tried to pull the tail of a huge serpent
that had fled into a cave. The mountains crumbled and everyone perished,
but a path of sorts was thus created between the two kingdoms.

Ancient China consisted of a large number of independent kingdoms. A
few centuries after Confucius, a ruler of Qin conquered Shu and the other
rival kingdoms and unified China for the first time. (It is in fact from 'Qin'
that the word 'China' derives.) His brief dynasty was followed by the long
Han dynasty (206 BC to AD 220), after which the empire split again, this
time into three kingdoms – Shu, Wu and Wei – each of which vainly
attempted to swallow the other two, ostensibly to return the country to the
peace and unity it had enjoyed under the Han. (It was only just before the
Tang dynasty, almost four centuries later, that the empire was once again
unified.)

The period of the Three Kingdoms is the basis of much chivalric legend
and romance built around several striking historical characters. These
include the great general Zhu-ge Liang, the so-called 'Chancellor of Shu',
who was one of Du Fu's particular heroes. Du Fu admired him for his
loyalty, strategic ability, astuteness and breadth of vision, and placed him
among the greatest soldiers and statesmen in history.

Zhu-ge Liang, living in retirement, was requested three times by the
adventurer Liu Bei (who considered himself the legitimate heir to the Han
empire) to act as his adviser before he finally consented and helped establish
Liu Bei as the First Ruler of the re-created Shu kingdom. Liu Bei on his
deathbed asked Zhu-ge Liang to set his own incapable son Liu Chan aside
and become emperor, but Zhu-ge Liang made Liu Chan the Second Ruler
and served him as loyally as he had served his father. In AD 228 Zhu-ge

Liang personally led a campaign against the kingdom of Wei, but he died
before it came to a decisive outcome.

Several shrines in Shu were dedicated to Zhu-ge Liang. In 'Thoughts on
an Ancient Site' the likeness referred to is his portrait in a temple in
Kuizhou. In 'The Chancellor of Shu' the shrine mentioned in the poem
stands outside the city walls of Chengdu, the capital of Sichuan. In 'The
Old Cypress Tree' the scene is again the temple in Kuizhou, but the
common shrine to Zhu-ge Liang and Liu Bei referred to in line 10 hearkens
back to Chengdu once more.

Li Bai lived in Shu for much of his youth; he moved here from Chinese
Turkestan when he was five. Du Fu lived in Shu in his old age and wrote
much of his greatest poetry here. Even today in Chengdu, his 'thatched hut'
is a much visited tourist spot.

11 *The Chancellor of Shu*
See note 10.

12 *An Autumn Meditation*
This is one of a group of eight meditations Du Fu wrote while recuperating
in Kuizhou. The chessboard is in fact a *go* board; the streets of Changan
were laid out in a square grid.

13 *The Old Cypress Tree at the Temple of Zhu-ge Liang*
See note 10.

14 *Grieving for the Young Prince*
The Dragon and the Son of Heaven are references to the Emperor.

The Shuo-fang veterans were the loyalist troops raised to defend the pass
that was the key to the capital. They were unwisely ordered to attack the
large rebel army of An Lushan rather than to hold the pass defensively. As
a result they were defeated, and the capital was laid open to the cavalry and
camelry of the rebels.

The Five Tombs mentioned in the last line of the poem refer to the tombs
of the early Tang emperors, the prince's ancestors.